Hey! That's My Fly!

by
Donald Stephen Caviness Jr

This book is designed to discuss with your preschooler at bedtime. Colorful hand painted pictures along with questions serve as aids for conversation about sharing.

Dedicated to my beautiful wife Carol, who has believed in me for three decades...I can't imagine why.

copyright 2013 Hanging Rock Publishing, LLC
www.TinyMouseStory.com
Like us on Facebook- "Tiny Mouse Story"

This is Cameron and Carmella. They like flies.

1) What type of animals are they?
2) What are they doing?

They can do this for hours.

1) Can you do this with your tongue?

2) Why or why not?

Now there's a problem!

1) What happened?
2) What do you think will happen next?

This could go on all day.

1) What are they doing?
2) What should they do?

It did go on all day.

1) Why are they still having trouble?
2) What would you do?

They awoke the next morning with sore tongues.

1) Why are their tongues sore?

2) Are they being stubborn?

"You should try sharing," said their Dad.

1) Why should they share?   3) Why is sharing important?

2) When have you shared?

"But there's only one fly!" they said.

1) Why aren't they sharing?
2) What things do you have trouble sharing?

"Really?" asked their father.

1) What do you see?

2) Why would it be easy to share?

3) What did Cameron and Carmella not think about?

"I am so sorry, I feel so selfish," they said to each other.

1) What have they done now?
2) Why?
3) Have you ever said I'm sorry?

1) What just happened?
2) What do you think they will do this time?
3) What might they have learned?
4) What would you do?

1) What did you enjoy about this story?

2) Who shares with you?

3) Do you think you will have more friends or fewer friends if you share with them?

Sharing is Fun!

Color me!

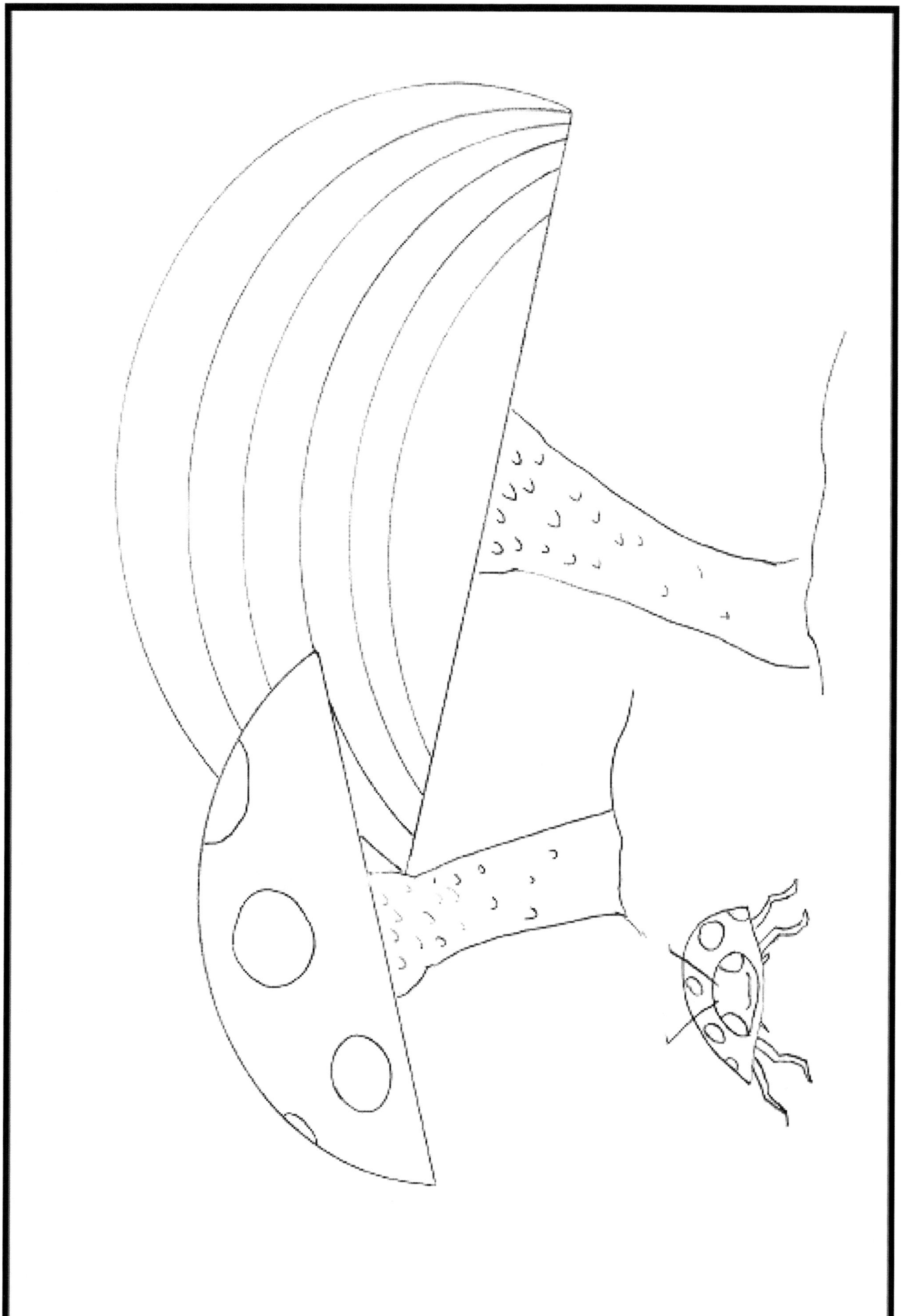

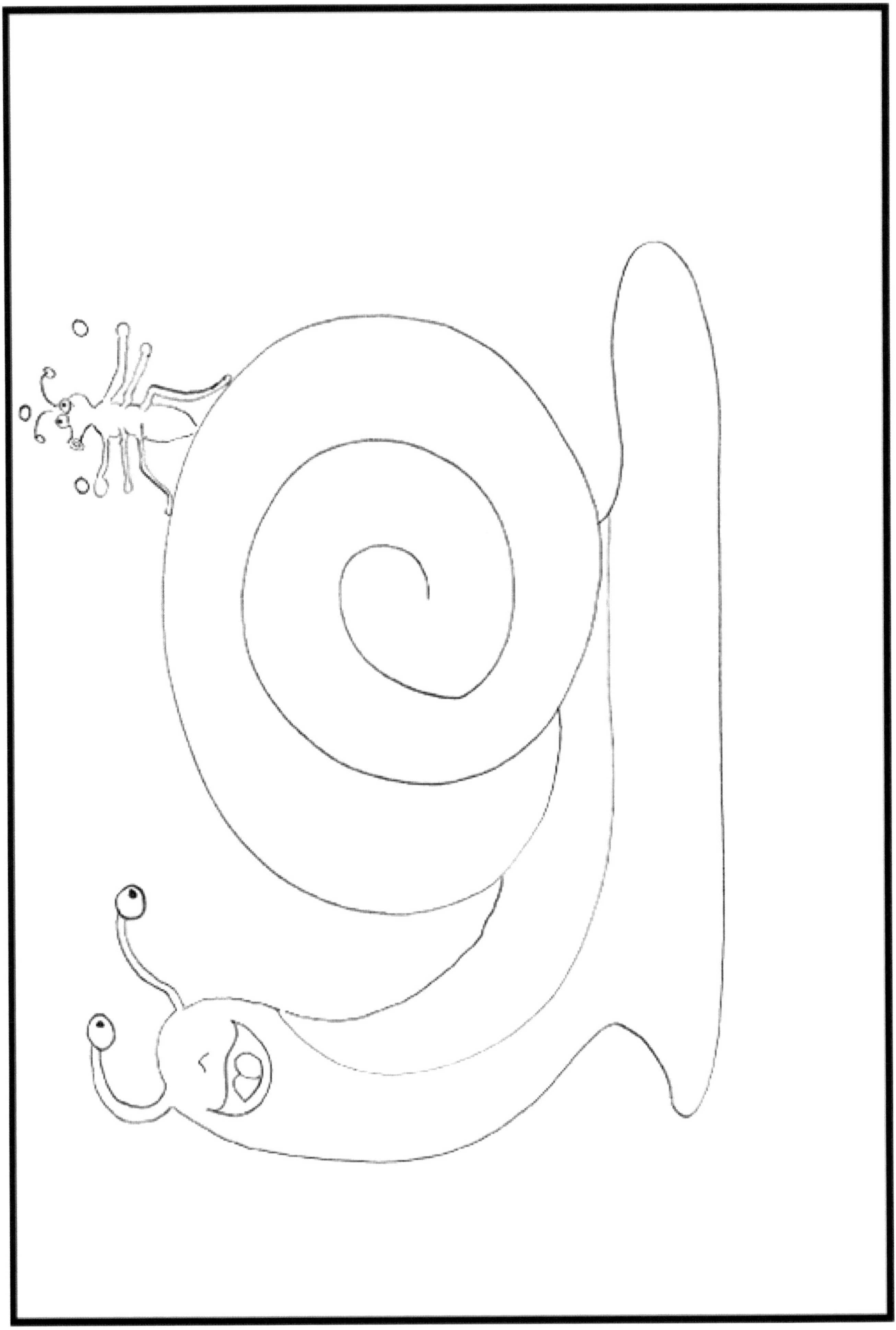

Draw me

Count the lollypops
1 through 5

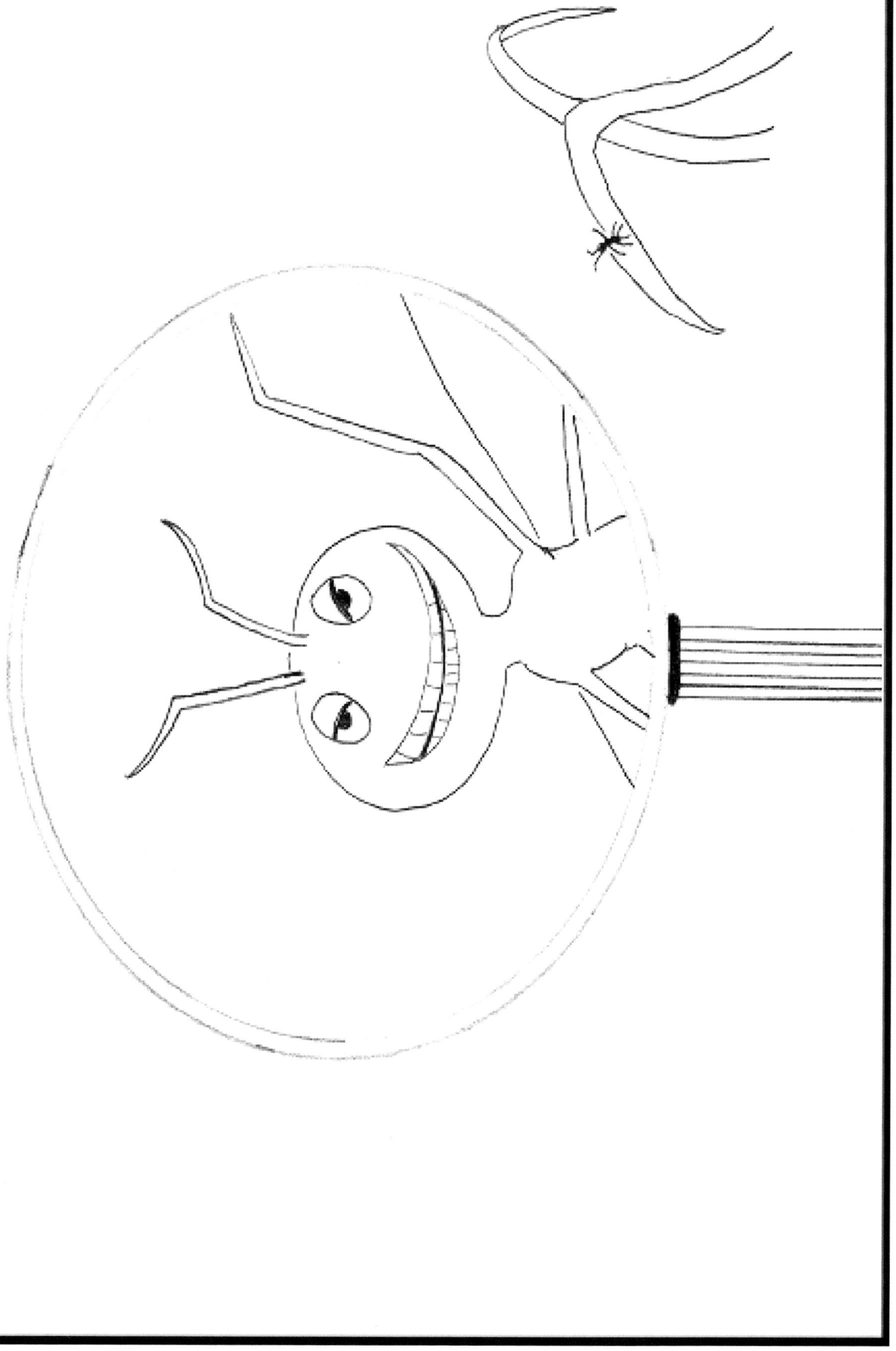

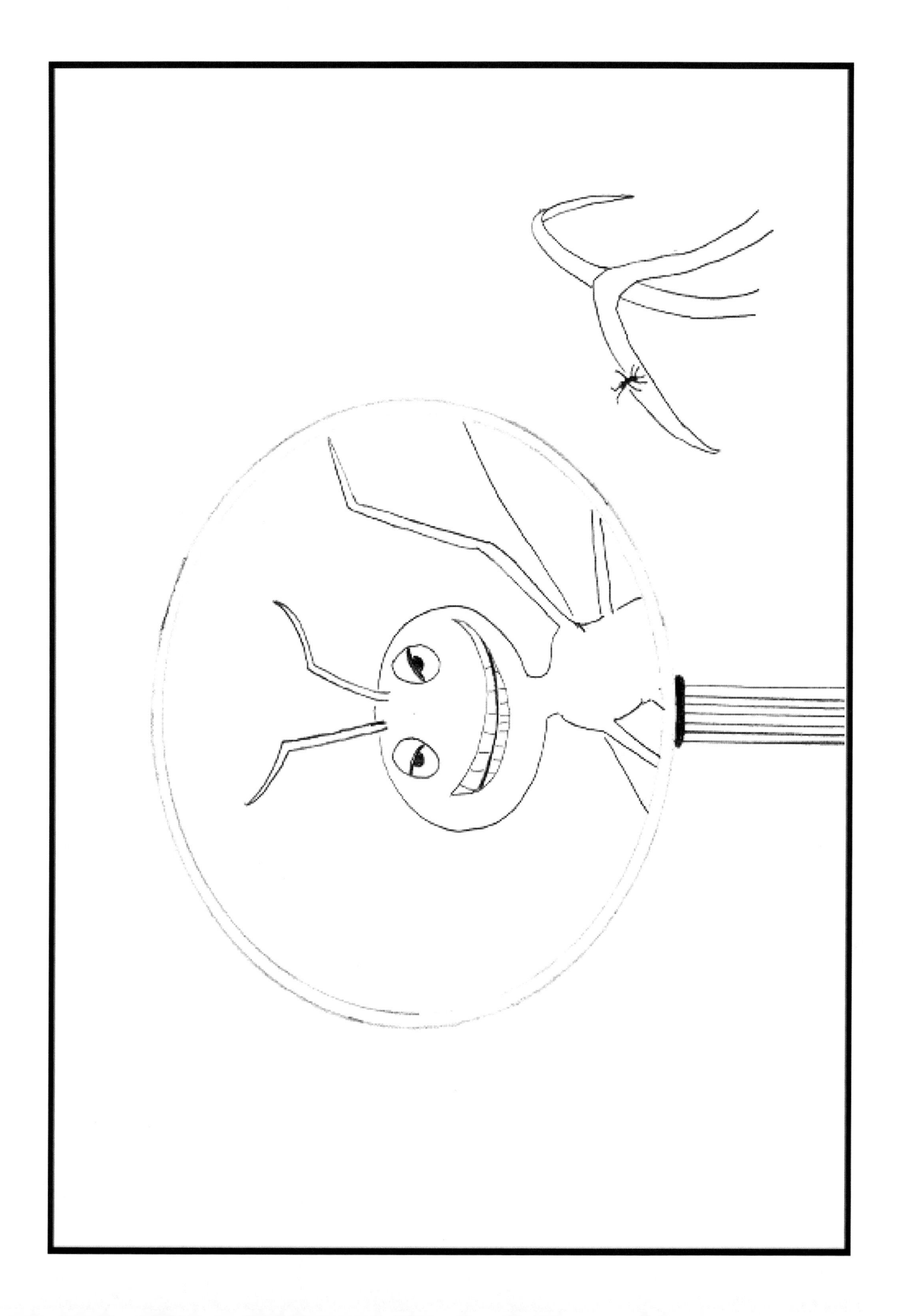

Draw me!

I want to be a butterfly. What would you like to be?

Draw us!
We like to sing. Will you sing with us?

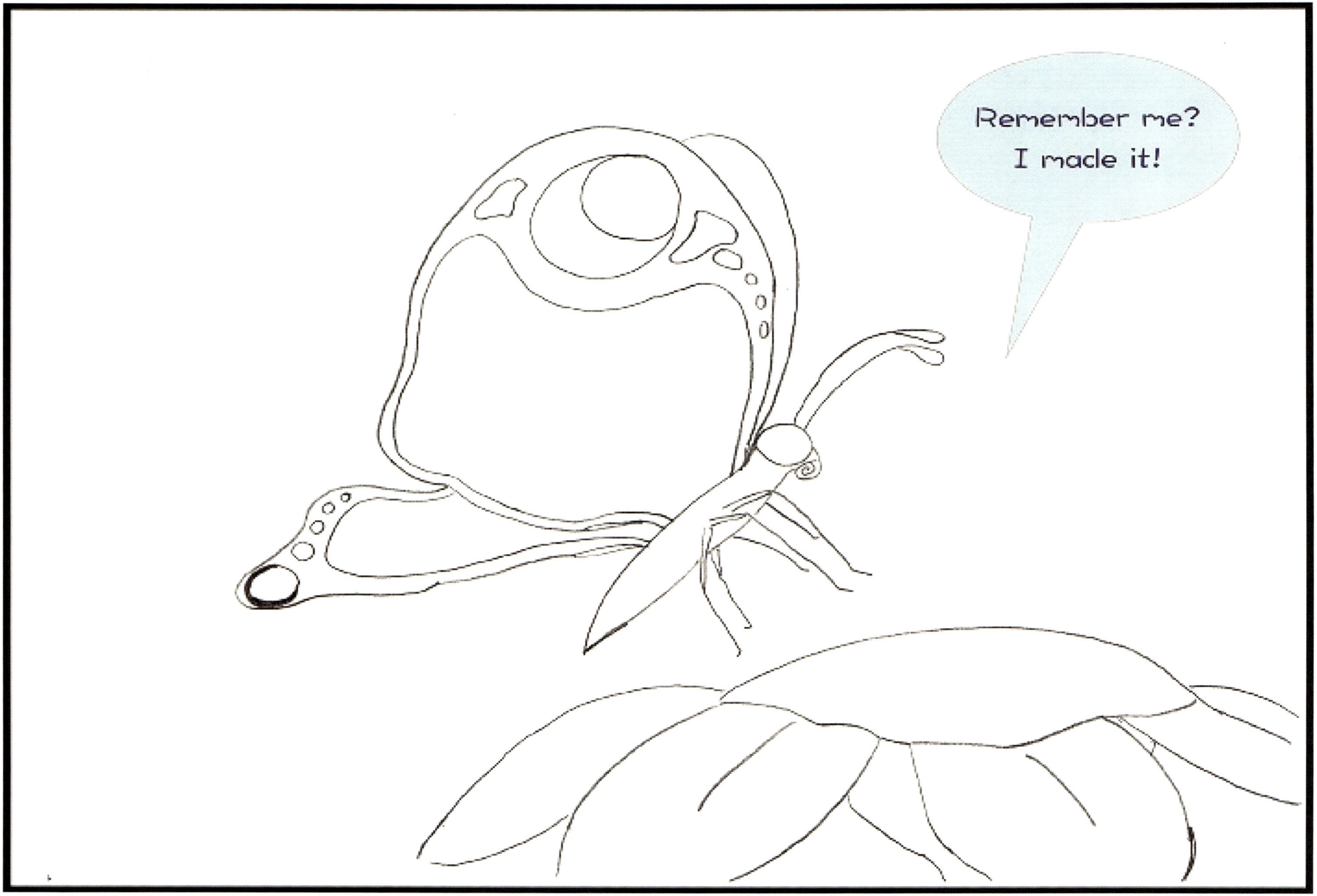
Remember me?
I made it!

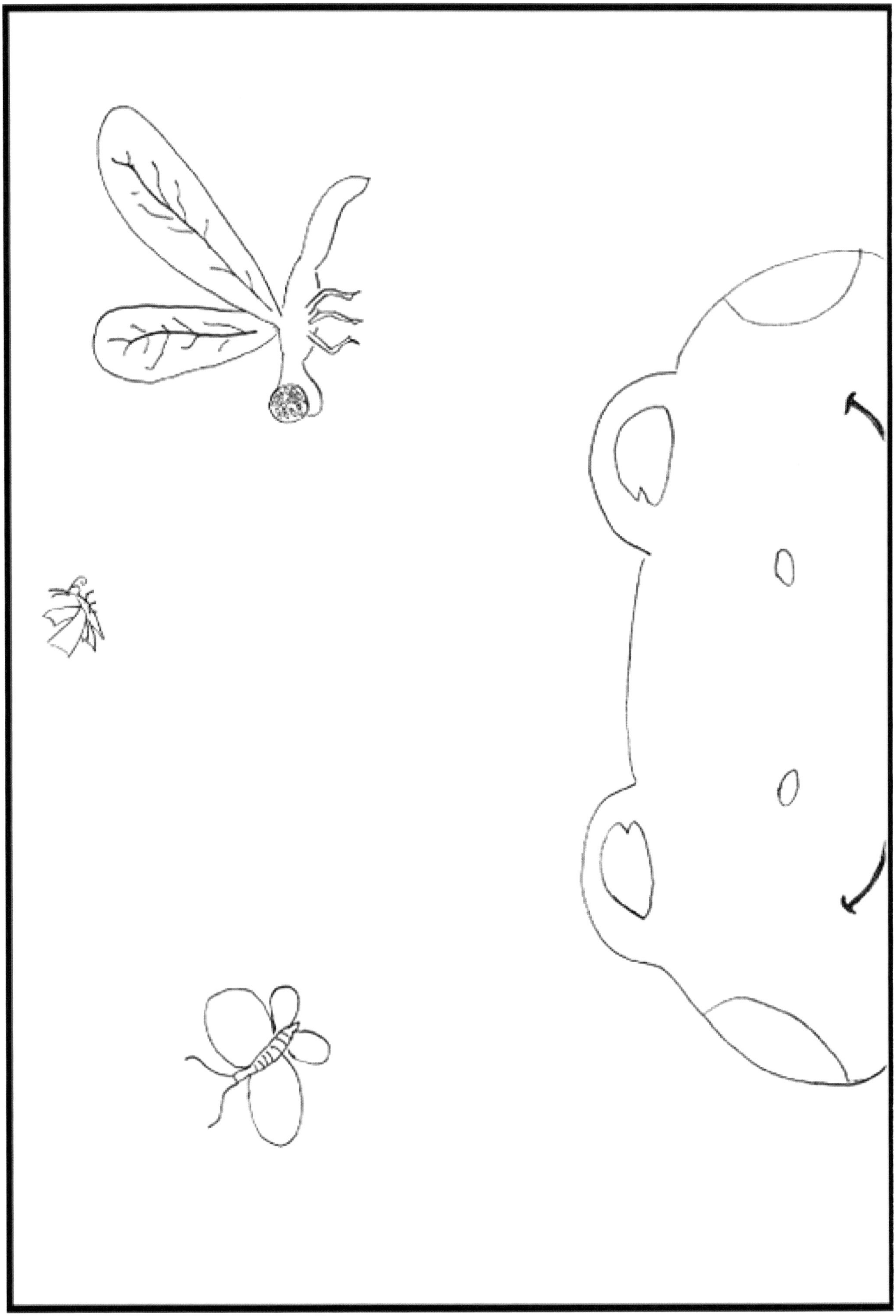

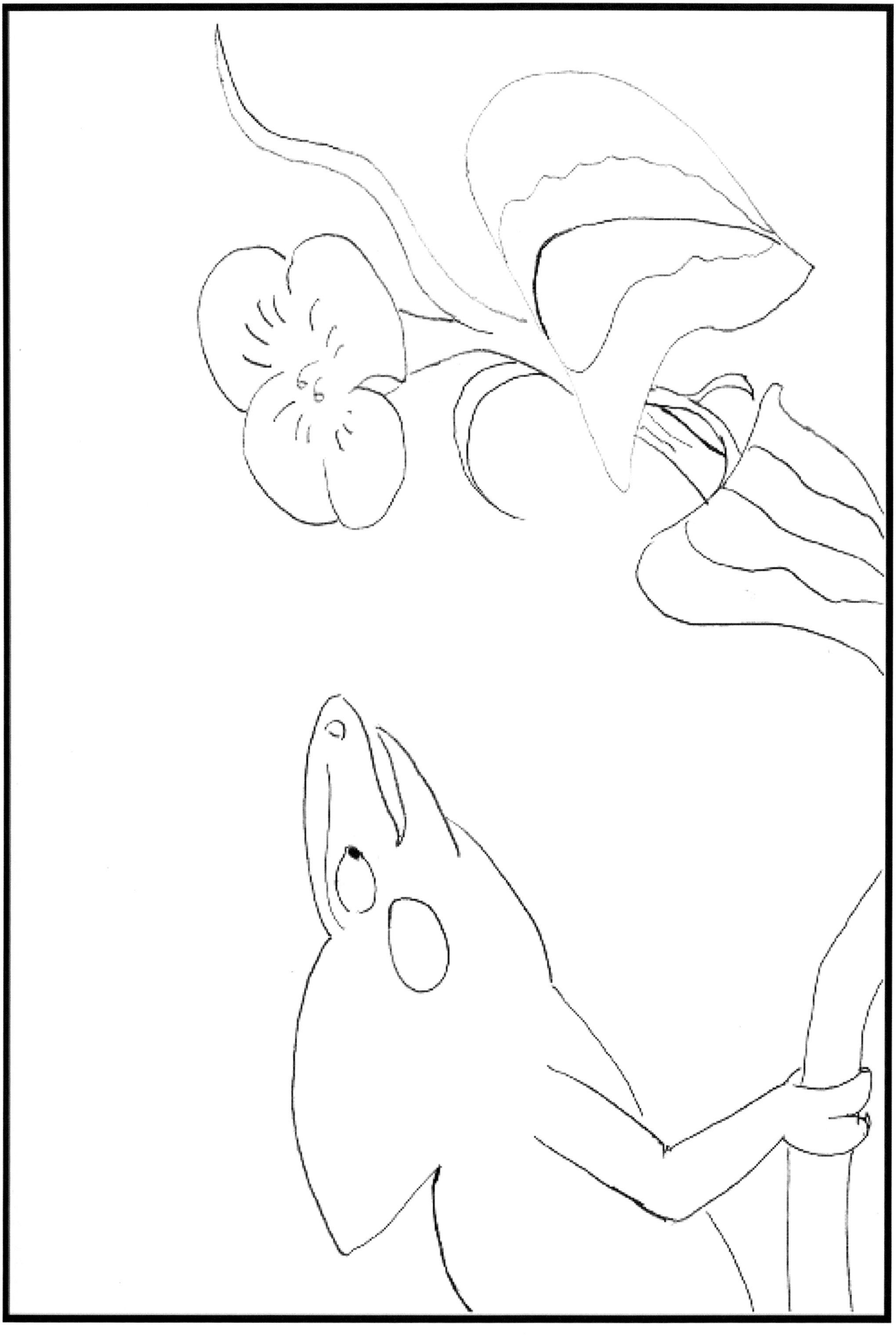